# Teach Me, Jesus

**Photographed and hand painted by Kathleen Francour**
**Stories by Sylvia Seymour**

Photography: © 1997 Kathleen Francour
Carefree, Arizona. All rights reserved.

ISBN: 0-7853-2123-3

PUBLICATIONS INTERNATIONAL, LTD.
7373 North Cicero Avenue
Lincolnwood, Illinois 60646

# The Vow

Chris and Rachel sat on Rachel's porch with their Sunday school class. "Jesus just touched people and made them well. That's pretty neat," Chris said to Rachel.

"Yes, and remember that He was always kind to everyone. He loved His friends, but He loved His enemies, too," said Rachel.

"Do you think His friends were like you and me?" asked Chris.

"I'm sure of it. I hope that I can be as good a friend as Jesus was," said Rachel.

"You're always kind and you always share. Only Jesus can do miracles, but YOU can promise to always be kind," said Chris.

"Jesus would like that. You are such a good friend. You are like Jesus, too," said Rachel.

By the prayers of Jesus, Lord teach us how to pray.
By the gifts of Jesus, Lord teach us how to give.
By the toils of Jesus, Lord teach us how to work.
By the love of Jesus, Lord teach us how to love.
By the cross of Jesus, Lord teach us how to live.

Good Lord,
Help me to win if I may,
and if I may not, help me to be a good loser.

Our Father, who art in heaven,
hallowed be Thy name.
Thy kingdom come,
Thy will be done, on earth
as it is in heaven.
Give us this day our daily bread;
and forgive us our trespasses,
as we forgive those who trespass against us;
and lead us not into temptation,
but deliver us from evil.
For Thine is the kingdom,
and the power, and the glory,
for ever and ever. Amen.

# A Baby Sister

"Benjamin, come meet your new baby sister," said Mother. All Benjamin could see was a blanket that wiggled. And it was Benjamin's blanket!

"Mommy, do I have to share ALL my things with the baby?" Benjamin pouted.

"You're a big brother now. Sharing and caring for your little sister is very important. See how small and helpless she is?" Benjamin peeked into the blanket and saw a tiny face and two little hands.

"Benjamin, can you hand me the baby's bottle? I think she's hungry."

Benjamin handed his mother the tiny bottle and curiously watched as the baby grabbed it with her dainty mouth.

"Thank you, Benjamin. You're such a good helper."

"Hmm, maybe a little sister's not so bad after all."

God be in my head,
and in my understanding.
God be in my eyes,
and in my looking.
God be in my mouth,
and in my speaking.
God be in my heart,
and in my thinking.
God be at my end,
and at my departing.

Please give me what I ask, dear Lord,
if You'd be glad about it.
But if You think it's not for me,
please help me do without it.

Help us to listen to Your voice.
Help us to be willing and quick
to do Your work.
Help us to be friendly and loving.
And help us to thank You every day
for all Your gifts to us.
Through Jesus Christ our Lord.

Amen.

# Two Bunny Ears

"I can't do it," Krista groaned. "MOMMY! I can't tie my shoelaces. Oh, Mommy, it's so hard."

"Let's ask Jesus to help you. Remember, He is watching you." They prayed together. "Now, take the lace and make a bunny ear. Tie it around and pull it through. Look, there are two bunny ears."

Krista laughed. "Let me try. Make a bunny ear. Tie it around…wait, wait. Make a bunny ear. Tie it around…. Make a bunny ear. Tie it around and…pull it through. I did it, Mommy, I did it! Thank you, Jesus!"

Dear God,
Be good to me.
The sea is so wide,
and my boat is so small.

All for You, dear God,
everything I do, or think,
or say, the whole day long.
Help me to be good.

Lord of the loving heart,
May mine be loving, too.
Lord of the gentle hands,
May mine be gentle, too.
Lord of the willing feet,
May mine be willing, too.
So may I grow more like Thee
In all I say and do.

Dear Lord, teach this child to pray,
and then accept my prayer.
You hear all the words I say
for You are everywhere.